Scottish Folds Cats as Pets

A Complete Ultimate Guide

Facts & Information, where to buy, health, diet, lifespan, types, breeding, care and more!

By Lolly Brown

Foreword

You might be surprised to know that all, yes, all Scottish Folds share the same ancestry to the original one found somewhere near a farm in Coupar Angus in Perthshire, Scotland, was taken in and lovingly named Susie by its owners in the 60s.

Susie eventually had kittens and two of them had folded ears just like hers which was kind of a curious oddity. Cat-fancier and farm-neighbor William Ross was fortunate enough to adopt, register and start breeding Susie's kitten. Hence our present enjoyment of this domesticated feline.

Given the proper care and love, Scottish Folds could share many fun-filled years with you. Their loving nature is popular amongst many since many of these felines are inclined to become quite attached to their guardians.

Find out more about these literally well-rounded cats and decide if you are worthy and ready to add one to your household.

Table of Contents

Chapter One: Introduction

Most cats are said to be aloof and independent therefore many people who are just as independent choose to take in cats instead of dogs as pets.

Here is where the Scottish Fold stands apart. Its unusual distinctive physical appearance and its loving nature make it a popular choice for many cat lovers and have changed the mind of many dog lovers about felines.

The Scottish Fold is a breed of cat that is said to be quite different in character from others. Due to a dominant gene the Scottish Fold looks a tad unusual from the rest because of its folded ears, giving it an owl-like appearance.

Once you decide to make a long term commitment of owning a pet, keep in mind that owning a feline would mean you are ready to give and provide for its needs. Owning a pet doesn't come cheap and you will have to factor it into your daily routine as you will be responsible for its life and care. You will have to add the expense of their upkeep and health care into your monthly budget. No matter the breed, all cats need to be taken care of with utmost care. From nutrition, grooming and visiting the vet to monitor their health.

Consider yourself lucky if you were given a chance to adopt one of these adorable owlish-looking cats because Scottish Folds are significantly more in demand and quite expensive if you choose to buy one. It is mainly because of its rare genetic oddity which is responsible for their folded ears and rotund looking physique. Not only are they sought after for their unique look and breed - they are also popular because of their loving nature and their inclination to lovingly attach themselves to their owners.

However, caring for them requires more than your initial investment during acquisition. It will take time; loving care and quite a bit of effort on your part in integrate your new friend into the family.

No matter the breed you choose, adding a pet to the family requires commitment, time and a whole lot of love. Scottish Folds will need your daily attention to maintain cleanliness and overall good health. Brushing their teeth to avoid periodontal disease once a week would be better than no cleaning at all, but what would be ideal is to do this at least every other day if not daily. Combing through their fur once a week will help remove dead fur and distribute skin oils and will give both you and your new friend some much needed quality down time.

SFs are pretty sociable felines who like gentle play therefore they integrate well into families with little children. If you are a household with other pets, be them feline-friendly canines and/or other felines, you'd be tickled to know that SFs, with gentle introduction get on well with other pets.

It is recommended to keep Scottish Folds as indoor cats to avoid them from unwarranted violent attacks by larger animals, contracting disease from being in contact with feral cats and strays, as well as avoiding having them stolen - which has often been the case for many. Remember that genetic oddity that makes their ears fold over their head make them attractively different hence quite an eye-catcher to many who come across one.

When considering a pet for yourself or the family, it is imperative that you understand the type of feline you will be integrating into your home. This book aims to enlighten you in getting to learn about the Scottish Fold better. It sheds light and gives you informative, utilitarian and helpful tips in taking care of, socializing, grooming, feeding, and dealing with these docile cats.

This book shall also show you the benefits of taking in a Scottish Fold. A sweet cat who languishes on and adores attention, the Scottish Fold will normally want to participate and interact with people and children who extend love reverence toward it. You'll discover that it isn't one who likes to be left alone for extended lengths of time - so unless there are other people or pet friends at home it can socialize with whilst you're away, you may want to strongly consider if you are ready to take in a Scottish Fold.

The Scottish Fold is happiest when around its humans and would love nothing more than to visit with you and sit on your lap (or chest) as you lounge around watching the TV or enjoying a good book.

If you have read this far then you are possibly one of many who are in strong consideration of getting or adopting a Scottish Fold Cat. Read on further to find out more and this should hopefully help you come to a decision.

Glossary of Cat Terms

Abundism – Referring to a cat that has markings more prolific than is normal.

Acariasis – A type of mite infection.

ACF – Australian Cat Federation

Affix – A cattery name that follows the cat's registered name; cattery owner, not the breeder of the cat.

Agouti – A type of natural coloring pattern in which individual hairs have bands of light and dark coloring.

Ailurophile – A person who loves cats.

Albino – A type of genetic mutation which results in little to no pigmentation, in the eyes, skin, and coat.

Allbreed – Referring to a show that accepts all breeds or a judge who is qualified to judge all breeds.

Alley Cat – A non-pedigreed cat.

Alter – A desexed cat; a male cat that has been neutered or a female that has been spayed.

Amino Acid – The building blocks of protein; there are 22 types for cats, 11 of which can be synthesized and 11 which must come from the diet (see essential amino acid).

Anestrus – The period between estrus cycles in a female cat.

Any Other Variety (AOV) – A registered cat that doesn't conform to the breed standard.

ASH – American Shorthair, a breed of cat.

Back Cross – A type of breeding in which the offspring is mated back to the parent.

Balance – Referring to the cat's structure; proportional in accordance with the breed standard.

Barring – Describing the tabby's striped markings.

Base Color – The color of the coat.

Bicolor – A cat with patched color and white.

Blaze – A white coloring on the face, usually in the shape of an inverted V.

Bloodline – The pedigree of the cat.

Brindle – A type of coloring, a brownish or tawny coat with streaks of another color.

Castration – The surgical removal of a male cat's testicles.

Cat Show – An event where cats are shown and judged.

Cattery – A registered cat breeder; also, a place where cats may be boarded.

CFA – The Cat Fanciers Association.

Cobby – A compact body type.

Colony – A group of cats living wild outside.

Color Point – A type of coat pattern that is controlled by color point alleles; pigmentation on the tail, legs, face, and ears with an ivory or white coat.

Colostrum – The first milk produced by a lactating female; contains vital nutrients and antibodies.

Conformation – The degree to which a pedigreed cat adheres to the breed standard.

Cross Breed – The offspring produced by mating two distinct breeds.

Dam – The female parent.

Declawing – The surgical removal of the cat's claw and first toe joint.

Developed Breed – A breed that was developed through selective breeding and crossing with established breeds.

Down Hairs – The short, fine hairs closest to the body which keep the cat warm.

DSH – Domestic Shorthair.

Estrus – The reproductive cycle in female cats during which she becomes fertile and receptive to mating.

Fading Kitten Syndrome – Kittens that die within the first two weeks after birth; the cause is generally unknown.

Feral – A wild, untamed cat of domestic descent.

Gestation – Pregnancy; the period during which the fetuses develop in the female's uterus.

Guard Hairs – Coarse, outer hairs on the coat.

Harlequin – A type of coloring in which there are van markings of any color with the addition of small patches of the same color on the legs and body.

Inbreeding – The breeding of related cats within a closed group or breed.

Kibble – Another name for dry cat food.

Lilac – A type of coat color that is pale pinkish-gray.

Line – The pedigree of ancestors; family tree.

Litter – The name given to a group of kittens born at the same time from a single female.

Mask – A type of coloring seen on the face in some breeds.

Matts – Knots or tangles in the cat's fur.

Mittens – White markings on the feet of a cat.

Moggie – Another name for a mixed breed cat.

Mutation – A change in the DNA of a cell.

Muzzle – The nose and jaws of an animal.

Natural Breed – A breed that developed without selective breeding or the assistance of humans.

Neutering – Desexing a male cat.

Open Show – A show in which spectators are allowed to view the judging.

Pads – The thick skin on the bottom of the feet.

Particolor – A type of coloration in which there are markings of two or more distinct colors.

Patched – A type of coloration in which there is any solid color, tabby, or tortoiseshell color plus white.

Pedigree – A purebred cat; the cat's papers showing its family history.

Pet Quality – A cat that is not deemed of high enough standard to be shown or bred.

Piebald – A cat with white patches of fur.

Points – Also color points; markings of contrasting color on the face, ears, legs, and tail.

Pricked – Referring to ears that sit upright.

Purebred – A pedigreed cat.

Queen – An intact female cat.

Roman Nose – A type of nose shape with a bump or arch.

Scruff – The loose skin on the back of a cat's neck.

Selective Breeding – A method of modifying or improving a breed by choosing cats with desirable traits.

Senior – A cat that is more than 5 but less than 7 years old.

Sire – The male parent of a cat.

Solid – Also self; a cat with a single coat color.

Spay – Desexing a female cat.

Stud – An intact male cat.

Tabby – A type of coat pattern consisting of a contrasting color over a ground color.

Tom Cat – An intact male cat.

Tortoiseshell – A type of coat pattern consisting of a mosaic of red or cream and another base color.

Tri-Color – A type of coat pattern consisting of three distinct colors in the coat.

Tuxedo – A black and white cat.

Unaltered – A cat that has not been desexed.

Chapter Two: Scottish Fold Cats in Focus

The Scottish Fold breed is recognized by some of the most renowned cat-fanciers association in the United States and the world, like The International Cat Association (TCA), American Cat Fanciers Association (ACFA), the Cat Aficionado Association (CAA) and Cat Fanciers' Association (CFA) today.

As mentioned earlier in this book, Scottish Folds are felines who get on well with people, are able to easily integrate themselves into families big or small. It easily manages to share love and attention with other cat-friendly pets and its humans and is one of the most sociable cats with one of the sweetest, quietest voice you'd ever hear.

What to Know About the Scottish Fold

All Scottish Folds today come from one lineage - a white cat, whose ears curiously had unusual folds in the middle and who earned its keep around a farm by keeping mice at bay. She was lovingly called Susie by her guardians. When Susie gave birth to a litter of kittens and two were born with her same folded ears, William Ross, a neighbor and cat fancier was fortunate enough to have been able to adopt one of the kittens. He with the help of Pat Turner, a geneticist had started to breed Scottish Fold kittens.

Scottish Folds have varied names depending on registries made. Scottish Folds sporting longer fur are known as Scottish Fold Longhair, Coupari, Longhair Fold and Highland Fold.

Scottish Folds are definitely not high maintenance cats when it comes to grooming. A regular nail trimming every week and ear cleaning when it needs one as well as a daily brush - teeth, which is - would be all it would need.

With support and gentle introduction they integrate easily with other cats and cat-friendly dogs. So if you are thinking of inviting another pet in your home, the Scottish Fold is definitely a feline you'd want to ponder.

Quick Facts

Pedigree: Cat Fanciers' Association

AKC Group: Scottish Fold

Breed Size: Medium,

Height: 10-15 inches (25-38 cm) tall

Weight: 8-12 lbs for females and 8 lbs. for males

Coat Texture: short, medium to long

Color: Bluecream, White, Blue, Cream, Red, Silver, Cameo, Brown, Black, Tortoiseshell others sport patterns of Tricolor/Calico, Tabby, Bicolor, Ticking, Shaded, Spots and Smoke

Eyes: expressively round close-set eyes that could be in hues of green, blue and gold.

Ears: folded ears drooping toward face giving it a rounded appearance

Tail: if mishandled or injured the Scottish Folds tail could develop painful stiffness and great discomfort

Temperament: it needs moderate attention and loves being around and interacting with its humans

Strangers: sociable

Other Pets: with the caregivers patient integration it readily adapts to other cat friendly pets you may own

Training: Highly trainable and adapts easily to people who handle them gently

Exercise Needs: frequent, lively exercise is strongly encouraged for Scottish Folds to lessen limb injuries due to being overweight.

Health Conditions: Scottish Folds are prone to cardiomyopathy and polycystic kidney disease

Lifespan: typical average lifespan is 15-16 years

History of Scottish Fold Cats

In the 1960s, the first discovered barnyard cat, Susie - who earned her keep as mouse-patrol, had a litter of kittens and two happened to sport Susie's same rounded, droopy, folded ears. One of Susie's offspring was first registered by its adoptive caregiver, William Ross, with the Governing Council of the Cat Fancy (GCCF) and was given its name, the Scottish Fold in 1966. He, along with geneticist, Pat Turner had started breeding them. They discovered those of the litter who had folded-ears only began to become apparent on the third or fourth week. They also learnt that not all Scottish Folds had folded ears. As they progressed they noticed that some if not half or more of the litter had unfolded ears. It still had shared the same roundish tip but instead of drooping toward its face it didn't.

It was discovered that because of a dominant gene, passed on from parents both with folded ears, a Fold could be prone to the degenerative bone disease, *osteodystrophy*. That if left undiagnosed will cause great distress on your cat and its caregiver.

76 kittens were birthed in the first three years of the program. Only 42 out of the lot had folded ears and the rest sported unfolded ears. It became apparent to them that an

incomplete dominant gene in some of these owlish looking cats was the reason of the ear mutation which caused the ears to fold forward toward its face giving it a roundish appearance.

However, due to painful limb and tail deformities - which was found out much later to be due to inbreeding - its registry was revoked in 1971 and was refused showing in Europe. Many of the cat-governing councils also supposed that the feline was prone to ear infections and ear mites because of its triple folded ears which drooped toward its face.

The dedicated Rosses were bent on getting the Scottish Fold its rightful recognition. They realized that in order for them to do that they would have to think larger and bigger. Farther even. It dawned on them that reclaiming recognition for the Scottish Fold and the possibility of working on better breeding practices and procedures would only be possible if they took the cats to another country.

It was only when the Scottish Fold found its way to the shores of the United States did great improvement of breeding become noticeable. It was observed and learnt that the best mate for a successfully healthy litter of a Scottish Fold cat was to cross breed the Scottish Fold another breed of cat. The most successful method, still employed by many upstanding breeders, was to mate a Fold with either a British Shorthair or an American Shorthair. The litters birthed from this method showed less of the genetic disorder that can be passed down to the next generation if improperly bred.

This was an opportunity to take a closer look at what the Scottish Fold cat was like. It became apparent how easily it could adapt to and share space with other cats and even some select cat-friendly dogs. With watchful eyes and loving observation guardians and caregivers became aware that the mild temperament of the Scottish Fold cat did not depend on whether it had folded or unfolded ears. They observed that whether or not a Scottish Fold cat had folded ears, they all shared a calm aura about them. Time and experience showed the diversity of fur, patterns and colours of the Scottish Fold cat varied greatly.

More importantly the results of extensive monitoring and recordkeeping showed that crossbreeding with a British or American Shorthair was one of the best ways to avert a population of Scottish Fold cats that could potentially live a painful existence and silently suffer from osteodystrophy.

Once this was established breeders were better equipped with knowledge and facilities to create a conducive atmosphere for the cats. Litters then started showing less and less limb and tail deformities. And much was learnt about the habits, the medical issues, personalities and traits of the Scottish Fold.

It was Salle Wolfe Peters, a renowned Manx breeder from Pennsylvania who was later credited for establishing this stronger and less prone to congenital disorder breed.

The Cat Fanciers Association (CFA) granted it recognition in 1973 and was awarded championship status in 1978. Another milestone was reached for the Scottish Fold in the mid-1980s, when the long-haired Scottish Fold was given recognition by the same Association.

Whilst looking for a Scottish Fold, keep in mind that there are varied names for its kind, like; the Highland Fold or the Longhaired Fold.

All pedigreed Scottish Folds today come from one lineage - Susie, the first recorded white barnyard cat, whose ears curiously had unusual folds in the middle and who earned it's keep around a farm by keeping mice at bay. She was lovingly called so by her guardians, and farm owners, the McRae's. When Susie gave birth to a litter of kittens and two were born with her same folded ears, William Ross, a neighbor and cat fancier was fortunate enough to have been able to adopt one of the kittens which he named Snooks. He with the help of Pat Turner, a geneticist had started to breed Scottish Fold kittens.

Because of limb and tail deformities due to a genetic abnormality which could render a Scottish Fold to suffer from osteodystrophy, its registry with the Governing Council of the Cat Fancy (GCCF) was revoked. It has not been recognized since.

Happily enough, once the Scottish Fold, a kitten of Snooks, crossed the pond and found its way to the United States, did its tendency to develop osteodystrophy greatly lessen. Years of diligent study showed that the manner of how the Scottish Fold were bred improved and the occurrence of the painful deformity an SF can be prone to if born of inbred (or two folded-eared) parents weighed a big factor to the good health of a litter of Folds.

Chapter Three: Scottish Fold Cat Requirements

Compatibility of pet and guardian is crucial when choosing to take in a pet for yourself or your family. Dynamics have to be considered as well as easy transition and integration. Research is important at this point of you making a decision.

Hereafter you will find information about what it takes to be caregiver and guardian to a Scottish Fold.

What Are The Pros and Cons of a Scottish Fold?

Get to know the breed and sort of the pet you choose to take in. It is sound to determine if you are ready to take on the responsibility for the care of one. In this short section you will find information about the positive and negative sides to acquiring or adopting a Scottish Fold.

Pros

- Amiable and mild-tempered
- It integrates well with its caregivers
- It is friendly and sociable to cat-friendly pets you already have
- Quiet with a soft voice and hardly makes a fuss.

Cons

- They are prone to cardiomyopathy and polycystic kidney disease
- Their tails tend to develop painful arthritis if handled roughly

Cat License Requirements

If you are planning to acquire a Scottish Fold as your pet, there are certain restrictions and regulations that you need to be aware of. Licensing requirements for pets varies in different countries, regions, and states.

In the United States there are no federal requirements for licensing either cats or dogs – these rules are regulated at the state level. While it is true that most states do not have a mandatory requirement for people to license their cats, it is always a good idea to do so because it will not only serve as protection for your pet but also for you.

Here are some things you need to know regarding the acquirement of Scottish Fold cats both in United States and in Great Britain.

United States Licensing for Cats

The average annual license cost is $10.00. Cat licenses for senior citizens are $5.00. Costs may vary depending on state, and may change without prior notice.

When you acquire license for your cat you will be given a cat number that can then be linked to your contact information. If your cat gets lost and someone finds it, its license can be used to track you down so that they'll be able to return to you your pet. Of course, this information will only be available if your cat wears a collar with an ID tag.

It is also ideal that four month old cats and up as well

as indoor cats should still have a license because it is required by municipal law. Even those cats that never leave the house have a way of getting out through accidentally open doors, gates, or windows. Also, a natural disaster like an earthquake or fire may cause your pet to flee the safety of your property; having your Scottish Fold cat licensed will help reunite your lost pet with you.

If you want to apply for a cat license, you can search the website of your municipal or state government online. You will be able to download the application form and just follow the procedure. After filling up the form, you can mail it to their office together with a fee, in some states there is currently no fee for a cat license so make sure to check first and find out how much it cost.

Documentary requirements must be submitted before permanently getting a pet license. They are as follows:

- Residents must include the current rabies certificate,
- Proof of spay and neuter, and microchip (if applicable) to make the license current.

In most states, these are the main documents needed to get a cat license. There might be additional requirements that need to be submitted in other states. The license will be considered temporary status until all documents are received.

If you don't want to put a collar on your cat a good alternative option is to have it micro-chipped. A microchip serves the same function but they can be embedded under your cat's skin so that it won't be lost. The procedure for having your cat micro-chipped is very quick and painless.

Great Britain Licensing for Cats

In Great Britain, licensing requirements for pets are a little different than they are in the United States. There are no overarching licensing requirements for cats in the Great Britain but you will need to get a special permit if you plan to travel with your cat into or out of the country.

Your cat may also be subject to a quarantine period to make sure he isn't carrying a disease like rabies – rabies has been eradicated from Great Britain through safety measures like these so it is important to maintain them.

Should You Opt for More Than One Scottish Fold?

Scottish Folds are amiable felines and enjoy the company of other Folds. Folds tend to get along better when they grow up together, so if you are seriously considering on getting more than one, a pair is a manageable together. Pairs who've live together have been observed to be moderately independent of each other but will enjoy the company of the other when playtime is the order of the day.

You will find out more about integrating a Fold into your home in the following chapters. But remember that if you have an established Scottish Fold at home, you will still need to act as mediator during induction. Felines are by nature territorial beings and may show signs of anxiety or distress when they sniff out a stranger, be it human or of the four-legged sort, enter their premises.

You can cushion this situation and gently integrate the new Fold with the established Scottish Fold with detailed tips you can find in this chapter.

That being said, a Scottish Fold does enjoy being around their human caregivers and will be ready to shower its guardians with all the love and affection your heart can take. So if you are the busy cat-lover who has to be at a million different places at once and can't be there for your furry friend at most times of the day then it would certainly be ideal to give your Scottish Fold cat the company of another.

Do Scottish Folds Get Along Well with Other Pets?

If you are the sort of guardian who has more than one established pet and is thinking of adding one more, the Scottish Fold is one you would want to consider. Many pet lovers keep their minds open about adding pets into their homes. Pet guardians with existing pets worry about integration of new pets into homes with established pets. Sadly many often make the mistake of not doing the proper research they need to do before bringing home a new addition into their homes. This can be a cause of great frustration and exhaustive effort.

If you were to prepare yourself, to study the pros and cons and to ask the right questions then the milestone of integrating your new Scottish Fold to your established pets won't be too much of a task.

Most felines - like most pets on four legs - are territorial animals. They tend to take stock of their boundaries and stake claim of spaces and areas as they become familiar with a new place.

During initial meeting and integration of pets you will notice a bit of tension and excitement in the air. It may cause a bit of a commotion at the onset of the meeting or a lot of curious sniffing at the very least. Your patience and supervision at this point is absolutely crucial.

If you are a family with existing pets you'd be glad to know that Scottish Fold cats are known to get along well with other cat-friendly pets. A chill-out Javanese, a playful Pomeranian, a laid-back Basset Hound, a Black and Tan Coonhound who thrives and dotes on companionship, or a gentle Newfoundland giant, are just some cat-friendly dogs who would be more than willing to share space and attention with a Scottish Fold.

Scottish Folds are docile, sweet-tempered, relaxed and highly clever cats. They easily get along with other pets and are able to accustom themselves to new accommodations, and guardians, with ease and panache. Your assistance is crucial at this point. With patience and mindful integration you'll find them to easily blend in well with other cat-friendly pets you may already have at home.

When Introducing a Scottish Fold In a Household with another Cat - and Vice Versa

If you are a household with an existing feline pet, then you probably have already noticed that most felines are quite territorial. They like to stake their claim on spaces around the home and will seem agitated when another pet or strange human is in the home.

Give your old feline buddy sufficient time to get used to the new Scottish Fold if you choose to add one to your family. Here are some useful tips you can employ to make the transition fuss-free.

- Allow the cats to get used to the new scent - to literally sniff each other out. Ideally, you should place the new cat inside a room and allow the established cat to smell their new roommate from the other side of the door. Provide the established cat a piece of clothing or blanket the new cat was in contact with recently to sniff out. Gently set this near the established cat and give it time to investigate this new scent and allow it time to help it get used to the smell.

- You can start the next phase of introduction and place them both in the same room but in strategically different corners. With your supervision and the aide of another family member, sit and observe how they act and react upon seeing each other. Per chance that you are doing the integration on your own, utilize a cat carrier to allow the established pet to get closer to the new one.

- With the aid of an indoor fence, place both cats in the space with the indoor fence acting as barricade. Observe the body language of both. Watch how each of the cats act and react around each other. You will know that the barricade can be eliminated altogether when they are relaxed and calm with the others presence.

- As soon as the walls come down and they are in the same space with no boundaries and seem calm around each other, you can start encouraging the next phase which is play. Take a feather-teaser and just start by slowly moving it from side to side, up and down. This will definitely get both of their attention and you will soon see that with gentle play they have overcome a small milestone down a long road of a happy relationship.

- Make sure you would have provided separate and identical feeding bowls and water dishes, and place them in separate areas of the same room where they can enjoy meals together but with a respectable distance between them.

- Provide them with separate identical beds in the same room. There is nothing more a feline dislikes than feeling less important. Providing them with identical beds allows them to share and switch it up when they feel like it.

- Just like us two-legged folk, our four-legged furry-faced friends require separate toothbrushes. There is a reason why toothbrushes are personal, and that is the spread of mouth infections and could be transmitted through sharing toothbrushes. Invest on a good pet toothbrush for each of your pets' oral hygiene.

- The ideal ratio of litter box to cat should be 2:1. This may seem a tad much to you, but again, this is something you need to know before you make your decision to add to the lot. Cats are by nature very iffy about doing natures business in a dirty box. More so are they iffy about doing their business where another just went - which could lead to agitation and constipation. Provide the cats clean litter boxes around the home where it is visible to them. Introduce them to the areas especially when they look like they are about to do their business or posing to urinate. Remember to regularly clean the litter boxes as cats hate going in a dirty box.

- You may provide a soft hypoallergenic blanket they can both share and romp in for a little exercise or a game of Hide and go Seek. This can be a good source of exercise for cats as they have a penchant for hiding, sneaking up on and playfully lunging at their buddies and guardians. A nice, clean, fluffy blanket is like a playground for felines. And it doubles up as a good nap place for tuckered out kitties.

- There are many other things your cats can share apart from a place in your heart like, beds (they may opt to interchange, or sometimes cuddle) and toys (one may favor a piece of toy more and the other may take a liking to another).

- They will usually be curious and may interchange feeding and drinking bowls too. This is why to avoid having one feel less important than the other or to avert the feeling of insecurity (yes, cats are perceptive animals) it is recommended to purchase and provide identical feeding and drinking bowls.

- You will want to create for your Scottish Fold separate perches for each of them. Strategically position these perches around the room to avert your cats from perching on high bookshelves or curio cabinets. You may have to train them to use their perch instead of on top of the refrigerator. You can make the perches at home by recycling some old wood and attaching them onto walls with wall brackets. Make sure the perches are braced and attached to the walls well and are sturdy making sure that jumps on and off the perch is safe. Test out that the perch you make for your cat doesn't dislodge to avoid any spills or falling accidents.

- Like in any family, conflict may be something that you will need to mediate later. When meditating it is best to draw attention away from the conflict by clapping loudly and calling out to your warring feline buddies. You may also opt to use a spray water bottle to separate the two hotheads and allow them both some time out to cool off.

- Cats in conflict will usually look to their caregivers for conflict-resolution. A good way to remove the tension is to groom both cats at the same time. Give it equal attention and care as you do and speak to both while you does so. This is a good time to break out the brush and give them a calm brush-massage as you speak to them in calm loving tones.

Here's a piece of useful information you may want to refer back to later. If you are introducing a new cat into a home with an established Scottish Fold Cat, then half the job of integration has already done itself. With its easy-going attitude and its tendency for companionship, you'll soon find out that the Scottish Fold cat is also a welcoming one. Its friendly nature makes it one of the best candidates for The New Buddy Award and will warm up easily to a new pet addition to the family.

How Much Does it Cost to take in a Scottish Fold?

Having a new member join the household surely entails a shift in the monthly budget. Although Scottish Folds require very little maintenance other than the daily brushing of teeth, occasional cleaning of the ears, coat brushing and nail trimming, it will require inoculation and periodic visits to the vet.

If you are thinking of buying a Scottish Fold kitten, it could set you back anywhere from $400-$600 and this price hikes up considerably more if your SF is provided by a reputable breeder and bred in a high-end cattery. Factor in inoculation fees, transportation costs (if cat is being sent in from a remote location) as well as its initial visit to the vet.

This section of the book aims to help determine if you are financially ready to take in and be caregiver of an SF. Here you'll find an overview and a rundown of what you could be spending on a Scottish Fold should you choose to add one to your blend. This list will include vet care, medicine, food, treats and toys, grooming and sleep equipment as well as feeding and hygiene supplies.

Initial Costs

On average a Scottish Fold from a reputable breeder and cattery would cost anywhere from $600-$800. Note that you want to find an honest breeder as this will save you money in the long run. Unscrupulous breeders can potentially pass on genetically ill cats bred of parents who both carry the dominant gene. This will result in future medical bills and avoidable health issues for the cat. You will read more about the importance of knowing the history of your Scottish Fold as you read further.

Factor in initial inoculation, neutering, toys and grooming supplies. Otherwise, keeping your Scottish Fold indoors - save for the daily outdoor stretch, sunshine and exercise - would save you and your SF the headache of contracting disease from feral cats, or unwanted attacks from other animals.

Adding a pet to the family is almost equal to caring for a child - sans the schooling, tuition and back talk. So factor in these things as you consider which breed of pet is best suitable for your family and your finance.

Chapter Four: Acquiring Your Very Own Scottish Fold

Scottish Folds are funny cats who have a way of making you burst out laughing or giggling with delight. They have certain mannerism which may seem quite different if you compare them to other felines. It isn't unusual to find your Scottish Fold rest on its belly with its front paws snuggly tucked under them. Or you may walk in on their nap and find them splayed on their backs with their bellies in the air as they snooze.

To deprive a Scottish Fold attention is very hard to do and you will find yourself looking forward to getting back to them on days when you aren't at home. It will be very hard for you to not talk about your Fold to friends and family because they are a sort who can get into some mild mischief and will keep you in stitches.

They are a bunch of playfully curious felines who loves your attention. This is evidenced by an endless supply of hours upon hours of cat videos. With more being uploaded everyday it is clear testament that it may well be cats that break the Internet. Cats on video are as close as you can get to seeing pure joy with the naked eye. And the Scottish Fold breed has certainly carved a niche in the internet as a lovable cat that is clever, intelligent, sweet and soft spoken.

Now that you have come this far and have read much of what you need to know about the Scottish Fold, it's time for you to find a reputable breeder who you know will hand over a healthy Scottish Fold to your eager, waiting arms.

That is one milestone you will certainly cherish and remember as a good day. You will never be the same again after you meet your Scottish Fold. Its mild demeanor and its easy going, relaxed manner of moving about may just influence and encourage you to put on the brakes and chill out for a few. Its lifestyle of contented may just inspire you to reassess how you measure happiness. Its friendly disposition may just remind you to smile a little more. Its innocence may draw you to the simpler things in life that hold the essence of your existence together. The Scottish Fold won't only change the way you live your everyday life, its presence in one's life may just be the better option to soothe frayed nerves and everyday worries.

In this chapter you'll find out where to acquire or adopt a Scottish Fold in the pink of health, or if you are one with a big heart and deep pockets. Also included in this chapter is how to cat-proof your home.

Where Should You Acquire a Scottish Fold?

You'll find there are a number of ways for you to get a Scottish Fold into your life. You can certainly go to your local pet store and inquire if they have one. But keep in mind that there are other places than the corner pet store where you can get your Scottish Fold.

There are breeders in and around your area or close to you who sell them too. Do your research. Ask around and make sure that you only deal with a reputable breeder who isn't just out to make a quick buck. Don't forget to first consider looking into pet shelters before you dole out tons of cash. You won't only be saving yourself a pretty sum, you'll also be rescuing an animal that will for a long time will share with you its love and gratitude, change your life and add essence to it.

What to Remember When Choosing a Reputable Breeder

First off, be sure that you deal with a trustworthy breeder as it minimizes the woes of taking in an ill kitten.

Here are some tips on finding an honest Scottish Fold breeder:

- Gather as much information as you can about and get referrals for a Scottish Fold. Network and be in contact with groomers, pet shops and veterinary clinics.

- Research breeders with websites and scrutinize their ranking, reputation and license.

- Ask questions. And as lots of them. You need to make sure you have done the proper research to know you are not being taken for a ride. It will also help you find out which sort of Scottish Breed (fur-wise) you'd be ready for.

- Inquire of and about the breeder's program and what they use as well as their procedure to produce the kittens they market. Don't hesitate to ask assurances the breeder takes to eliminate or at the very least avert the transmission of some congenital conditions to the kittens

- Immediately remove breeders from your list who give dodgy, flowery, shady, and seemingly uninformed answers. Take care that you deal only with those who have been reputed to be humane in dealing with the breeding process.

- Immediately eliminate those from your list those who refuse to answer questions you have about the history, health, procedures or anything related to the welfare and future overall well-being of the kitten.

- Take a road trip and visit the breeder's facilities if you are permitted. See for yourself and check out if the shelter kept clean. Transparency and willingness to attend to and answer questions of possible owners is a positive and should be marked for strong consideration.

- Finances will be discussed so don't forget what terms the breeder has to offer. Once you have made a decision find out immediately about the breeders terms and make an agreement.

- Should you opt to buy a Scottish Fold kitten place a deposit to reserve your kitten – in the next section you will receive tips for choosing a kitten from a litter.

Adopt a Scottish Fold from a Rescue

Apart from dissuading fly-by-night, shady breeders, thinking about adopting from a shelter will cover you for doing a good deed of rescuing a Scottish Fold in need of a home. This is a choice with little financial investment but one that will give back for a long time. The benefits of adopting one are insurmountable and you just might be lucky enough to find one waiting for you at a shelter close by.

One obvious and distinct difference of acquiring a Scottish Fold from a breeder to rescuing one from a shelter is with the latter you'd have given it a chance of being in a better home - one that it deserves. It may also be house trained and housebroken which leaves you more room to get to know and get it integrated within the house as with yourself and your family. Remember that the Scottish Fold is one of the more mild-mannered of the feline specie and that getting them blended into your daily lives will be close to taking a walk in the park.

List of Websites of Breeders and Rescue Adoption

Scottish Fold Cat Breeders

TICA

<http://www.tica.org/find-a-breeder/item/315-scottish-fold-breeders>

TCFA

<http://cfa.org/Breeders.aspx>

Cat Breed

<http://www.catbreedslist.com/>

Rejinald Cattery

<http://www.vegasbrits.com/Scottish_fold_cats.html>

Cat Time

<http://cattime.com/cat-breeds/scottish-fold-cats#/slide/1>

Rescue Adoption

Petfinder
<https://www.petfinder.com/cat-breeds/Scottish-Fold>

Adopt a Pet
<http://www.adoptapet.com/s/scottish-fold-cats-for-adoption>

Homestead

<http://scottishfoldrescue.homestead.com/>

Rejinald Cattery

<http://www.vegasbrits.com/for_adoption.html>

Cat Time

<http://cattime.com/cat-breeds/scottish-fold-cats#/slide/1>

How to Select a Healthy Scottish Fold When Buying

You can count in a Scottish Fold into your family fold for as long 15 years and if well cared for even more, as you will find later as you read more. They are not susceptible to diseases most other felines are. This is when your decision making comes in. Your initial choices and tasks of finding out about the cat's history which you choose to adopt or acquire are of great importance and its future good health hinges on that.

The upkeep and maintenance of a Scottish Fold is minimal apart from its initial inoculation and periodical medical checkups, food and cat supplies and equipment. So be certain you have all bases covered before you bring home your Scottish Fold to ensure a happy, healthy and comfortable transition to its new home.

- **Behavior around Humans:** Mild-tempered and sociable, if a Scottish Fold displays aloofness or is skittish then it may have experienced abuse and or neglect from its previous owners. You may have to invest a bit more of time in integrating your new pet if this is the case. But with loving patience and a little bit of time, your new cat will understand and see you mean only good toward it and will warm up to you. Remember they are happiest and thrive best in a loving environment.

- **Mobility:** If you can check it in its present living conditions, do so. Have a see that the cat can walk well, is mobile and not in any way display signs of pain. Swelling of limbs is a telltale sign of osteopathy. If you choose to adopt one with some sort of injury or genetic condition then you should also be aware that you will be committing to medical bills and frequent visits to the vet.

- **Tail:** Scottish Folds tend to develop arthritis on their tail as they age. You'd easily know if the cat indeed suffers from it by lightly stroking its tail with the ball of your hand. Be gentle, should you need to test if it does show discomfort or pain. Gently, with almost feathered strokes, run the ball of your palm up and down their tail. If it does not avoid your touch or show agitation, the cat should be fine. If it does, your vet would be the best person to talk to about medication and care.

- **Cat-friendly Pet Interaction:** It will be necessary that you are present when you initially introduce the new addition to your family. Allow your new Scottish Fold buddy to roam and discover spaces around the house on its own hand, if allowed, supervise excursions out on your yard. Read more about pet-proofing your home. When introducing new pets to existing members of the family, make time for this milestone. This period will need the investment of a fraction of your time if done thoughtfully. Remember that there are some pets which are hostile toward others. You can avoid this situation and research if your present pet is a cat-friendly one. Your gentle patience will be rewarded with many years of loving, grateful affection. You will find out more about integrating pets in Chapter Six.

- **Appetite:** Scottish Folds have moderate appetites. Do not make the mistake of over feeding them as their genetic weakness falls on their limbs and may lead them to develop mobility problems and be in extreme pain.

- **Body Appearance**: Examine and scrutinize the fur, body, ears, and legs of the cat. Remember to be very gentle with its tail. Extreme and rough handling of its tail will cause medical issues to the cat.

- **Coat:** Gently look for ticks or fleas that the cat may exhibit. Scottish Folds have different fur length.

- **Skin**: Ideally, the cat's skin should be free from fungus patches and bald spots. If you choose to take on one it is best to have it confined and treated before introduction to your family and other possible pets you may have.

- **Eyes:** The round, expressive eyes of your Scottish Fold should be discharge free, clear and bright. Scottish Fold cats have the most expressive eyes that will be hard to refuse once your sights catch each other.

- **Ears:** Ears are to be wax free and clean. You want to watch out for tiny nicks or wounds that may get infected as well. It is imperative that the Scottish Folds ears are kept pristine to avoid ear infections. Be gentle when cleaning.

- **Mouth and Teeth:** Watch for any deformities or abnormalities like protruding teeth.

- **Belly or Stomach:** Check for swollenness or lumps around the belly area.

- **Anal Area:** Once again, and this is something stressed all the time when choosing to take in or buy a Scottish

Fold, gently lift its tail to check its anal area that it is clean.

Upstanding breeders only release Scottish Fold kittens at 12 weeks. It is strongly advised though that separation from mother is best kept off until the kitten has weaned off its mother. Hold off until the kitten is ready to eat solid kitten food until you take your home.

Chapter Five: Safety Tips to Remember Before You Take Home Your Scottish Fold

Assuming that you have already bought a Scottish Fold as your pet, the responsibility that comes with it is the most crucial part of the process. You as the owner, have to provide for its basic needs so that it will be healthy and happy.

In this chapter you will learn the different requirements needed for your cat such as its health requirements, accessories as well as how to keep it happy and healthy.

How to Safely Feline-Proof Your Home

Scottish Folds are amiable cats with a pleasant and docile temperament. And although they are pretty well-rounded cats, it is still important to know how to keep your new ward safe as its new guardian and vice versa. Read on to find out how you can start preparing your home to welcome your new found friend.

Secure Your Family, Fort and Feline

- Secure food and store them in cupboards or stack them in a closed pantry. Make certain that any food moved out of the fridge or pantry is tightly covered or sealed in a spill-proof container.

- Cats have a natural tendency to scrounge, hunt and rummage for food. Avoid a mess caused by this innate habit of felines of tipping, spilling or pushing over things by making sure your trash cans are covered tightly and won't spill out in the event that it topples over.

- Cats will usually play with tiny objects that they can roll around and play with if they come across an object that captures their fancy. Make sure that medicine be kept out of their reach. Accidental ingestion is not a situation you want to deal with as there are many human medicines that can be dangerously toxic if not fatal to cats. Aspirin and paracetamol are some of the more dangerous pills that you should keep out of your cats reach. As a rule of thumb, keep all medication away from the reach of children and pets.

- Keep tiny valuables stored away if you notice your little fur ball is the kind of feline who likes to play with shiny things. You wouldn't want it to swallow something tiny and have it lodge in their throat. If this does happen it is important to get your feline to the vet as soon as possible.

- Look up first aid tips that you can employ should your pet have an emergency.

- It would benefit the safety of all if you keep wires folded or protected from unwanted gnawing which may lead to electrocution.

- Make sure that there are no loose strings from curtains or blinds, ropes or wire your Scottish Fold could get entangled in.

- Medication, paracetamol, aspirin and/or prescription drugs are to be stored away and hidden. The risk of having your cat ingest a meant-for-human pill is the last thing you want to happen as it can be fatal.

- Cleaning products you use to clean around the house contain many toxic chemicals which are poisonous and can cause dire harm your new friend. Avoid emergencies and keep all cleaning products stored away where your kitten can't see or find the products.

- If your cat is allowed to roam the house and its perimeter be sure that you cat-proof your garage as well. Cats like to perch on high places. Be sure there is no heavy equipment or tools that they could push over the edge which may hurt them or people in the home.

- Build a sturdy perch with some recycled wood (sanded and painted with non-toxic paint) braced on the wall with a couple of brackets. This should be introduced as an acceptable place to perch instead of a high cupboard. Make sure that the brackets are securely fastened and won't fall off when the cat jumps on or off the perch.

- Determine that the plants around your home are non-toxic to your Scottish Fold. Should there be any poisonous plants like calla lily or deadly nightshade that flank or surround your home, you may want to opt to replace, replant at away from your cats allowed spaces or barricade it. Poisoning from these toxic plants or harmful ingestion by cats is a very real medical concern. In the Glossary of Feline Terms you will find plants that pose serious health dangers to your cat. Be sure that you continue to research further for other plants that will be a danger to your cat.

- Remember that cats can get carried away when they are at play. It can be quite a handful too if you are dealing with more than one pet. To avoid possible electrocution when your cat is in a curious mood or when rough housing with their furry pals use plastic covers to cover up electric sockets. These are just some additional safety steps to take to make certain your home life isn't suddenly disrupted by a situation that could have been avoided.

- Some cats have a tendency to gnaw at string and electric wires mimic string. Cat-proof your wires with those nifty wire covers that'll dissuade them from chewing on a live wire. If your cat has a penchant for gnawing at wires, you best cover them up. Earphones and charger wires should be kept and stored away from where they can be discovered by your curious cat. You will save yourself a pretty penny replacing chargers and earphones in the long run.

There are a lot more tips that is listed within this book to keep your cat safe in your home. Continue and read on as this will not only benefit your feline, but you as well, so that you can keep your home intact family-safe.

Chapter Six: Nutritional Needs of Scottish Fold Cats

Feeding your Scottish Fold cats is not that complicated. However, its level of activity should be taken into consideration to meet its nutritional diet. They're not choosy eaters but it is highly recommended that cats, like many other pets, should be given the right amount of recommended food for a balanced nutrition because proper diet can lengthen the life expectancy of your cat.

In this section, you'll learn the majority of your pet's nutritional needs as well as feeding tips and foods that are good and harmful.

Food and Nourishment

Scottish Folds, like other felines, are meat-eaters. This is important to know and mind whilst pondering on your decision. If this is not adhered to then you and your cat may face a long road of frustration and/or harmful food experiment. You may think they are picky eaters, but once it shows no bad effects once it tries out something, stick with two or three varieties. A good rule of thumb is to try out small portions of US pet-approved food with them. Remember that weight, breed and hybrid factor into how they should be fed. It is best to consult with your vet and get sound advice on the portions you should set out for your Scottish addition.

In this section of the book we will discuss the food and nutrition of your Scottish Fold. It will tell you what to feed your cat to successfully raise it medically-sound. It shall remind you of what Scottish Fold can and can't eat. And give you a better insight on how to feed your new cat.

The Nutritional Needs of Scottish Fold Cats

Scottish Folds are meat-eaters. Its diet is limited and if not given the proper foods may seem like finicky eaters.

Its diet should be rich in protein, fats and meats. Scottish Folds don't respond well to carbohydrates so foods based with such are to be eliminated from your grocery list and your feline's diet.

Remember that Scottish Folds share ancestry with some of the larger wild cats you know of today. Wild cats are not vegetarians and neither is your Scottish Fold.

To curb frustration, like getting your Scottish Fold sick or spending insane amounts of money buying sacks of food it won't touch, you'll need to keep in mind that SFs need protein, meats and fats and that it has a limited diet.

They seem to thrive best on smaller portions during periodic times of the day. Be sure to check with your vet first as to how much food is the proper amount to give the cat. Once determined you should stick to this regimen. It may seem that you are underfeeding the cat but it works best for its health and happiness in the long run.

Their little cute faces, tummies and overall health depend on meat to allow it thrive better. Below is a list of what they can and can't consume.

Protein

Do not make the mistake of thinking it eats like you or your cat-friendly dog. If a person were to eat the amount of meat a Scottish Fold did that person would sure develop serious medical conditions but not so for our little kitty.

Be sure that introduce meats or meat-based products to lessen the impact of stress on guardian and cat.

Calcium

Do introduce calcium to your Scottish Fold kitten by giving it a little yogurt, cream or some cheese. Do NOT give it cow's milk as it has shown the Scottish Folds intolerance to it. Substitute calcium intake with yogurt, buttermilk or cream cheese instead.

Cereals

Mash up buckwheat, oats, whole grain and brown cereals to its meals.

Carbohydrates

It is imperative to know that Scottish Folds' do not respond well to carbohydrates. It will not refuse it -hence a false sense of security that if it eats it, it must be ok... No. Carbohydrates in their diet tend to cause them to become obese and develop diabetes. Remember to avoid carbohydrates in its diet at all costs.

Water

Just like you and I, cats need to drink to refresh themselves and quench their tiny parched throats. Make sure your cat is getting enough fresh water.

What Foods to Choose for Your Scottish Fold

Scottish Folds need protein and a lot of it. That much we know. In this section you will find out a little more about what other foods you can and shouldn't serve up to your own funny-furry-faced feline friend.

You can avoid the long process of finding out what your Scottish Fold prefers eating by introducing small amounts of different varieties at a time. If you opt to have backup canned meals for those busy days choose foods deemed acceptable by the American of Feed Control Officials.

A wiser choice as caregiver and guardian is to include cooking their meals when you cook yours. It isn't a tedious a process as you think it is and it ensures that you are feeding it food you have control over in terms of freshness, selection and preparation.

Not only will it ensure the nutritional balance, health and well-being of your Scottish Fold, you will also find that doing this will put less of a dent on your finances.

Feeding Your New Scottish Fold Kitten

It's important to note that Scottish Fold kittens will need calcium. However cow's milk, contrary to popular belief is not an ideal source of this vital nutrient it would need. Cow's milk often gives the Scottish Fold kitten intestinal troubles and does not process cow's milk well.

Instead, introduce and give your Scottish Fold kitten other dairy products like dollops of cream, yogurt or cheese two to three times a week at the beginning - increasing the amount and frequency you give it as it grows - on its own if the kitten will eat it plain. You can opt to mix in some boiled and finely chopped chicken breast to the yogurt or cream. Alternately you can mash cereals into the yogurt, cream or buttermilk.

This serving amount, given several (6-7) times throughout the day, three times a week, will meet and work great wonders for its calcium needs nutritionally.

It is also important for its diet to get nutrients from cereals like, buckwheat, brown rice or whole grain. Egg yolks are also a recommended staple to give your Scottish Fold cat or kitten two to three times as it grows. Find out more about allowed foods you should give to your growing Scottish Fold in the next section.

Feeding Your Growing Scottish Fold Kitten

As the kitten matures you will see slight shifts in its food interests. You will notice that your cat may now prefer lesser feedings and may even show disinterest toward the usual foods it used to gobble up happily. Your keen eye will tell you that this is the time when you will have to introduce meat to the kitten's diet.

You will know when the growing kitten is ready for additional foods in its meals. They will usually display less interest in the usual kitty-food you've been giving them and this will be a good cue for you to begin introducing meat along with the other foods mentioned before in this book. Refer back to what you can and can't feed your Scottish Fold if you don't remember or are unsure. Ask your vet about other acceptable grains and veggies which you can serve to your Scottish Fold - for variety and because some veggies are seasonal. Inquire about calcium intake and what food you can give to your Scottish Fold as it grows.

Continue to include cereals, wheat, oats and rich in calcium dairy products in your growing cat's diet as you start to introduce meats to its diet. Mix in a yolk of egg in its meals at least twice a week.

Acceptable meats include boiled chicken and beef. Unacceptable meats would be pork and lamb. For variety you may also opt to boil brown rice, whole grain wheat, cereals or buckwheat along with the cut of meat you.

A good source of its much needed iron-intake will come from liver. It is recommended that you give your Scottish Fold some liver with its meals at least once a month. Boil some liver in water. Once it is cooked, chop it up or run it through a food processor. Mix it with some boiled chicken or beef. You should opt to add a bit of oats and some boiled vegetables to the mix to give it a balanced diet.

As the Scottish Fold Cat grows you will notice that it's feeding radically reduces in terms of frequency. When once you had to set out fresh food 5-6 times a day, you will notice that this job will radically be cut in half as your Scottish Fold matures.

Feeding Your Grown Scottish Fold Cat

Most humans make the mistake of thinking that the Scottish Folds diet is not unlike ours. But there is a difference and it is good to know that Scottish Folds thrive best when fed nutritionally sound food whilst making sure it has a balanced diet. So as much as it will not eagerly run to a dish of vegetables it is wise to remember that incorporating a bit of allowed veggies like boiled cauliflower, green beans, carrots mashed in and mixed into boiled and chopped up meats like chicken or beef is required for it to enjoy a healthy life.

The beauty of preparing the food your cat at home is that you can do this when you cook for the family. You can even go on a weekend spree of cooking and prepare these dishes which you can cool, store and reheat for later consumption during the following week.

Not only will you be ensuring sanitation, freshness and quality control of what you feed your cat, you are also doing your finances a real solid by making this part of your daily or weekly home routine.

Opting for Canned Food

Here are some tips to consider if you opt to periodically substitute canned foods to home prepared foods. It is always good to research which foods have been approved by food security agencies.

Do not get carried away by marketing hype that tells you this and that but really is just out to make a buck. Canned food inspected by and approved of by food security agency boards are wise choices.

Opt to alternate canned foods with home-cooked meals only when necessary. Sometimes when adopting or buying a well-bred Scottish Fold its former guardians may have fed it canned foods which you will need to know off the bat. You may have to continue feeding it this way as you begin to incorporate food that you prepare at home or equally healthy and well balanced foods that are store-bought.

Chapter Seven: Living with Your New Scottish Fold

In this chapter, you will learn lots of tips on how to deal with your Scottish Fold cat once they step foot in your home. You'll learn how to train them, groom and clean them, and even get some tips if you'd like to maybe present them to others through joining cat shows. These things are essential in making your pet's lifestyle as fun and wonderful as it can be. It'll make you a better owner if you know your cat's strength and weaknesses.

Things to Remember Before You Bring Home Your Scottish Fold

Having read this far, you have come to know what responsibilities you will have when you bring home your Scottish Fold.

It is imperative to remember that taking in a pet is a great responsibility that requires your willingness to care for it no matter what. In terms of health the Scottish Fold Cat, as long as you do your research on its history, it is a low maintenance cat that would need very little medical attention as compared to other pets.

Lots of patience and love is needed when incorporating your new friend into the family is crucial at the beginning of the relationship. The idea of taking in or buying a pet may look and sound easier than it seems. Having read this far you understand that in any home dynamics, an addition means a period of adjustment. This with is why you are called guardian and caregiver - because the success of a peaceful integration will largely fall on your shoulders.

Empower yourself with basic information on how to provide a happy and healthy home life to your new Scottish Fold. This section shall guide you on how to outfit and set up spaces and areas for your cat and its everyday basic needs.

You will find out how to set areas around the house to accommodate your new family addition like toilet spaces, play areas, dining space. It will also remind you to create safe boundaries around your house where your cat is allowed to wander.

Activity and Habitat for Scottish Folds

Just like humans, every cat is different from each other in personality and character. And just like us each of them thrives in homes where they feel safe, loved, protected and cared for by their caregivers.

The Scottish Fold cat may be a mild-tempered, charming, amiable and easy-to-get-along-with feline but this doesn't mean that it couldn't get into mischief if physical stimulation with proper toys and props isn't employed on a regular basis.

It is advised to keep Scottish Folds as indoor cats and take supervised outdoor trips with you or another caregiver from your family. Their roundish physique makes them eye-catchers and head turners and may fall into the wrong hands if not careful. Yes, there is real "cat – nappers" out there.

This is also a good time to consider the greenery and foliage you have surrounding your home. Take care that you are aware of plants that the cat may munch on and give it serious medical repercussions.

Keeping Your Scottish Fold Cat Fit and Healthy

Make downtime playtime an engaging but gentle one. Since Scottish Fold Cats are less inclined to exercise on its own, it is up to you and people in your home to have frequent playtime with your new addition. Obesity is a real problem your Scottish Fold may suffer if not given the proper stimulation and exercise whilst at play.

Cats enjoy chasing lasers, teasers, bouncy balls and plush toys. These are some of the recommended toys for play rather than your bare hands. Since the Scottish Fold does have a genetic inclination to develop painful tail arthritis you want to avoid any unintentional injury to your feline.

A scratching post or two will eventually have to find its place in a few spots around your home unless you were looking to refurbish and introduce the clawed-effect on your favorite furniture. Refer back and read more about cat-proofing your home in Chapter Six.

Equipment You Need to Supply for Your Scottish Fold

Litter Boxes

Alongside properly integrating your new pet in your home you will have to give it spaces where it can go do its "business" - go potty that is. If your new cat is not housebroken, fear not because cats are possibly the easiest to train to go to the toilet where it's supposed to amongst pets.

You should place litter boxes in strategic areas of the house that aren't tucked away. A hidden but busy hallway, one under an indoor, toxic-free, preferably decorative plant, a corner in the family room or in the toilet are ideal places for litter boxes and for cats to do natures business.

Cat Litter

You have a world of choices for scented cat litter that will keep hygiene and odor in check.

Be sure to shovel out the litter boxes at least twice a day. There is nothing more than a cat hates than a litter box full of dump. The rule of thumb on the ratio of cats to litter boxes is 1:2. One cat two litter boxes, two cats, 4 litter boxes. This ensures that cats are comfortable and will have no qualms doing their business when nature calls. Remember to change cat litter regularly. This will depend on how often your cat goes to the toilet.

Cat Carrier

Scottish Folds are great in adapting to new environments around them therefore ideal companions on vacations. They show almost no stress to traveling and is able to acquaint itself to new surroundings with ease.

A sturdy cat-carrier is recommended for road trips, out-of-town forays and short excursions around the city.

Cat Brush

Invest on a good brush which will be very useful for down time bonding and to massage your cat. Moderately frequent brushing will also help get the cat's skin and fur oils circulating better. This allows its fur to remain silky-soft.

This will be an especially important part of your routine should you choose to own a long-haired Scottish Fold as the longer fur sort will definitely be prone to matting. You will need to keep your Scottish Fold cat's fur tangle-free with more frequent brushing.

Cat Toys

Plush balls to munch on or to throw around, soft toys to run and chase after, teasing-feathers, bells and a sturdy scratching post or two are in order to help the fun happen and exercise in check.

Cat Bed

Choose a nice, soft, warm and comfortable bed for your Scottish Fold cat to sleep, curl into, warm up in and just a personal space of its own to laze about. If you have a sun porch set out a soft mat there too - where it can soak in some rays and enjoy a nice breeze as you enjoy the day with it.

Food Dish

Rethink plastic feeding dishes and opt for ceramic or stainless bowls for their food and water.

Scratching post

All cats have a tendency to sharpen its claws and nails by scratching and clawing at things. To avoid and avert furniture destruction acquires a couple of scratching posts which you would want to strategically place in rooms around your home where the cat is allowed to roam.

Toothbrush

Ask a an experienced owner or a veterinarian of how to properly brush its teeth and be sure that you snag a toothbrush for your new house mate along with the other stuff you're already going to get.

Good to Know When Acquiring Cat Supplies

Don't scrimp on supplies and equipment your pet will need. Invest in sound products and tune out all the marketing hype. If you choose right, you could save a hefty sum in the long run. These will last them quite a while if you get the sturdier sort.

Ask around and get tips from other cat guardians on where to get sturdy equipment for your Scottish Fold. There will be many products that will boast of this and that but just won't make the cut in terms of durability or quality. Again, don't get carried away by the hype. Check out pet websites which sell pet products and read through the ratings and comments of their customers to get a better idea of the products they manufacture.

Pay mind that you read the labels of products you may consider buying for your pet. As much as there are many upstanding pet merchandize merchants, there are a number of pet product producers who are merely out to make money. Many of these pet equipment producers use low grade materials that do not pass quality standards. There are others which use chemicals that may pose a toxic threat to your Scottish Fold as well as your family. Another mistake you want to avoid is buying second hand equipment and supplies for your Scottish Fold. Remember that cats can get anxious about a strange scent in their midst. It is still best to get affordable, sturdy and new equipment your cat will need.

Yes, the responsibility of owning a pet entails a lot of details that require attention and action. But the fruit of your extensive research will give you some peace of mind.

Presenting Your Scottish Fold Cat

The Scottish Fold cat is a recognized breed for both the Cat Fanciers' Association (CFA) and The International Cat Association (TICA) which means that it is eligible for pedigreed show. Showing your cat can be a wonderful but challenging experience and it is also a great opportunity to spend more time with your cat, which could strengthen your bond. Learning how to show your cat properly can take time, so do not expect to win your first show.

This section will give you a highlight about the Scottish Fold breed standard and some general show guidelines.

Scottish Fold Cat Breed Standard

The Scottish Fold cat is a wild and unique breed that is accepted and recognized by the Cat Fanciers' Association (CFA), The International Cat Association (TICA), and American Cat Fanciers Association (ACFA).

The breed standards for each of these organizations vary but this section will give you the ideal and general guidelines on the Scottish Fold cat breed standard.

General Breed Standard

Head

- Must be rounded with a firm chin and jaw.
- Must have a well-rounded muzzle and whisker pads
- Must have a short neck that is proportionate to the head
- Males should have a prominent jowl and cheek

Coat

- For shorthair Scottish Folds, the coat should be dense, plush, soft, not flat, and the color may vary.
- For longhair Scottish Folds, the length of the coat must be medium to long hair. The face, and toe tufts as well as the ears must be clearly visible.

Body

- Medium in size, rounded, firm and well padded

- Should have short and coarse legs but should have no problems with mobility
- Toes should be well rounded, complete, and neat
- Must have a well-rounded appearance with medium bone

Eyes

- Eyes must have a sweet expression
- Must be large, well rounded and should be wide open

Ears

- The ears should be folded forward and downward
- It should be small, tightly fold.
- The tips should be rounded
- Should be set in a caplike fashion to show the rounded head

Legs

- Legs should be well-proportioned to body
- Should be short

Paws

- Round
- Toes should be five in front and four behind

- Prominent knuckles

Tail

- Tail's length medium to long
- Must be proportional to the body
- Should have a rounded tip, tapering tail preferred
- Tails should be flexible

Preparing Your Scottish Fold Cat for Show

Showing your Scottish Fold cat can be a wonderful experience but it can also be quite challenging. In order to ensure that your cat does well in the show, he needs to be a strong example of the breed standard. Make sure that you familiarized yourself with the rules and regulations for the particular show in which you plan to enter your cat.

In addition to making sure that your cat meets the qualifications of the breed standard, there are also some general things you can do to prepare for a cat show.

Here are some tips to help prepare you and your cat for show:

- Make sure your cat is properly pedigreed according to the regulations of the show – you may need to present your cat's papers as proof so be sure to have them ready.

- Make sure to fill out the registration form correctly, providing all of the necessary details, and turn it in on time – you may also have to pay an entry fee at this time.

- Clip your Scottish Fold cat's claws before the show – declawed cats are allowed as well without penalty.

- Make sure that your cat is registered with the organization running the show.

- Be sure to enter your cat in the proper age bracket or category - some organizations allow kittens as young as 3 months.

- Find out what is provided by the show and what you need to bring yourself – some competitions provide an exhibition cage but you will need to bring some things.

Important reminder:

Below are the lists of things you need before the show:

- Your cat's pedigree and registration papers.
- Veterinary records and proof of vaccinations.
- Litter pan and cat litter (if not provided).
- Food treats, and food/water bowls.
- Cage curtains and clips to hang them.
- A blanket or bed for the cage.
- Any necessary grooming equipment, nail clippers.
- Confirmation slip received at entry.
- Food, water, and extra clothes for yourself.
- Garbage bag for clean-up.

Be prepared to spend all day at the show and bring with you everything you and your cat need to make it through the day. Some shows provide a list of recommended materials to bring so pay close attention to all of the information the show gives you with your registration.

Chapter Eight: Breeding Your Scottish Folds

Let's revisit the Dame of all Scottish Fold Cats today. Our old friend Susie's parents were never identified nor was there any record of the union which resulted to her. Hence, the oddity of the demure-looking, inward-folded ears of the Scottish Fold was for a long while a mystery.

No one knew why some of Susie's kittens had folded ears and others didn't and so this beautifully strange diversity piqued the interest of breeders. The results of many of the breeding then were unsuccessful and many resulted in kittens which displayed a congenital form of painful degenerative arthritis.

It slowly became apparent that inbreeding greatly affected the limbs and tails of these cats. Although a non-life threatening disease, if you are a lover of these furry critters, you'd not want to see your Scottish Fold in pain. Rather, if you are seriously considering adopting a grown cat who may display this congenital abnormality, accept that you shall be incurring medical bills to help soothe them when they display signs of pain.

There are those who would say that the Scottish Fold is a result of spontaneous mutation. Others would argue that breeding and human intervention play a big factor in the favorable results of minimizing the genetic limb and tail arthritis. The author would have to agree that both are correct. Remember, Susie's parents were never recorded and studies have shown that inbreeding is the culprit of osteodystrophy.

Your Scottish Fold should be bred in a humane and thoughtful manner. Any upstanding breeder should be transparent about their methods and should be eager to share information you need to hear about the Scottish Fold you are looking to buy or adopt. Never deal with a breeder who isn't ready to answer questions about cat history, their methods of breeding and the procedures they employ.

How to Properly Breed Your Scottish Fold - History Counts

Upstanding breeders will only breed a Scottish Fold with an American or a British Shorthair. Studies have shown that, although susceptible to osteodystrophy as a Scottish Fold ages, this passed-down genetic abnormality is greatly reduced and increases the chances of a healthy cat, only if outbred with a Shorthair.

That is to say, a Scottish Fold Cat should not breed, or mate, with another Scottish Fold Cat. Scottish Folds that both have the folded-ear gene will usually yield a litter of mostly folded-eared cats. However, they are least likely to survive for long. Or if they do, they live with painful deformities in their limbs and/or tail and will likely experience degenerative osteodystrophy throughout its life.

The British or American Shorthair doesn't have the mutant folded-ear gene and its robust physique seems to overwrite and prevent the genetic disorder from being passed to offsprings.

MFEO - Made for Each Other

The Scottish Fold is best out-bred with a British or an American Shorthair. Extensive study has shown time and again that the risk of contracting the genetic bone disorder, osteodystrophy radically lessens when this method of breeding is applied.

This is a vital part of selection to reduce the risk of passing on the genetic abnormalities it is prone to future generations to allow them a long, happy and pain-free life. Certain selected traits in the cats are carefully identified by upstanding breeders before the breeding process is begun. This drastically lessens the incidence of the genetic disorder being passed on to the next generation of Scottish Folds.

To Multiply or Not

At this point of your research you have learnt important things to consider when buying or adopting a Scottish Fold Cat. The same thought and study should be employed should you want to add little kitties to the lot at home. Make certain that you are aided by a licensed expert, a certified professional breeder.

At the onset of your quest to become caregiver to more of these adorably sweet felines, seek the advice of an experienced guardian. A seasoned caregiver who owns a healthy Scottish Fold Cat will be able to point out people you can start talking to about breeding your SF.

Chapter Nine: Keeping Your Scottish Fold Healthy

Scottish Fold Cats, like any other breed of feline or canine, can be prone to some illnesses, which can be avoided or at the least managed. Do more of your own research and thoroughly read through and refer to this section which has vital information that you will need to know to keep your new cat healthy.

It is imperative that you know what you are committing to when taking in or acquiring a cat. Part of this responsibility includes for you to find out about illnesses or medical conditions to which your Scottish Fold is and may be prone. It will be up to you as her trusted caregiver to recognize signs of distress, discomfort, unease or pain your Scottish Fold may display.

Your role and the parts your family plays as guardians are keys to a Scottish Folds healthy and happy well-being. Although many reports would say that a Scottish Fold lives up to about 13-15 years, there have been a number of reports as well of Scottish Folds living long happy lives of up to 17-18 years. With the proper care from its guardians the Scottish Fold will thrive and live in contentment surrounded in an environment of overflowing with love and warm companionship.

This chapter hopes to carefully illustrate what you need to look out for, measures you need to take and what you should do (or not do) to keep your Scottish Fold in the pink of health.

Breeding Manner Matters

Without getting into too much technicality, this is one thing you need to know straight up; the manner of how the Scottish Fold is bred have strict guidelines to be followed to avoid a genetic disfiguration that can be quite painful for the feline. Humane and upstanding breeders will tell you right away that breeding a Scottish Fold with another will result in genetic issues that will haunt the cat throughout its life that could lead to debilitating pain. If your Scottish Fold, once playful and mobile, displays lethargy or unwillingness to play, see your vet immediately.

Responsible breeders would never mate two cats with the same folded ear gene, so they are normally - rather, should instead be - mated with a British or an American Shorthair.

Breeding two cats with the folded-ear gene will almost certainly result in debilitating osteodystrophy. This is a congenital, non-treatable, genetic and painful condition that causes deformities in the legs, tail and the vertebrae of the cat. It causes them pain and discomfort. And should this be the unfortunate case of one, the genetic disorder will only be apparent later on as it matures. This is why it is important to know how the kitten will be or was bred.

If a kitten is born of parents who both have the folded ear gene, it displays symptoms of osteodystrophy about 4-6 months into its life.

Symptoms of Osteodystrophy:

- Tail is short and thick

- Bones which are affected may appear thicker

- Bones affected are tender to the touch

- Cat does not jump or avoids jumping (be observant)

- Play time may be difficult for the kitten

- Limping may follow

- As the cat ages as as the disorder worsens it may look like they are walking on stiff-outward-sticking legs

- Movement may slow down and lack of coordination may be apparent

- Seeming tiredness and lacks desire to move about

- Severe pain

These are some pretty avoidable heartache that you can avoid if you deal with the right breeders. Transparency at the onset of your search for your new house companion needs to be thorough.

If you choose to take on an ailing Scottish Feline, bless your heart. You should know however, that you need to be ready for its medical care which equates to a major shift in your weekly and monthly financial allotments.

Cleaning Your Scottish Fold's Ears and Eye

Contrary to popular belief, Scottish Fold cats aren't as prone to ear mites and ear infections like other cats are. But a gentle cleaning of its triple folded ears on a weekly basis is strongly recommended. This avoids buildup of dirt and wax and is a good time to check for mites. When doing so, take a pad of cotton and moisten it with a 50-50 mixture of warm water and cider vinegar. Lift up the fold of the ears gently and lightly wipe the insides of its ears. This is best incorporated to your downtime with the cat when both of you are relaxed.

Don't neglect that its eyes need cleaning too. To clean the eyes of your Scottish Fold you need only to gently wipe its eyes with a soft cloth moistened in warm water. Be sure that use separate parts of the cloth to wipe each eye to avoid irritation or the spread of infection.

Grooming Your Scottish Fold

The furs of the Scottish Fold Cat, because of crossbreeding, come in long and short kinds with unique patterns or one solid color. Frequency of grooming will then depend on whether you choose a short-haired or long-haired Scottish Fold. Its bits of information like these you want to know before procurement as you research. It is essential at this point because you want to know what you need to factor into your time.

Scottish Folds with short fur - at a minimum - should be brushed once a week. If you'd prefer to take in one with long hair, then brushing should be done at least thrice a week to prevent matting and tangling of its fur. The long-haired sort will need much more brushing attention as it will be prone to matting and clumping. Brushing will ensure that essential oils are distributed throughout its skin evenly and will keep its coat soft and shiny. Brushing your Scottish Fold is also a good time to investigate if it has fleas. If it does unfortunately contract fleas or mites, consult with your vet on what soap or shampoo is best for the situation.

It was advised at the beginning of this book that Scottish Folds should be kept as indoor cats, but should you allow it the daily supervised foray out into your yard, give it a gentle brushing at least thrice a week to remove debris it may have picked up during its time outside.

Trimming Your Scottish Folds' Nails

To trim or not to trim, has become a big question when it comes to clipping your cats' nails. Since you will probably want to keep your Scottish Fold indoors you'd want to give it a once-a-month or when-needed nail trimming. Just like you you'd want to do this for purposes of hygiene. You also want to avoid major scratching damage to your furniture when nature takes over and your Scottish Folds' instincts tell it to sharpen its claws on your favorite lounge chair.

Take its paw and gently press on it to reveal each nail. The rule of thumb is to clip a wee above the pink line. To keep a squiggling cat from getting cut too far into its skin and to secure the other paws, some people have found that swaddling the cat in a warm blanket while doing this makes it safer for cat and guardian to carry out the task. The blanket seems to allow them a bit of comfort during a manicure. Which, observation has proved, they don't really enjoy. This is not to say that this is true for all cats. You will be come to discover a technique best for you and your Scottish Fold as you get to know each other.

Proper Oral Hygiene for Your Scottish Fold

This won't be a popular activity for your Scottish Fold but one that should be managed. Brush your cat's teeth with mild toothpaste and a toothbrush specifically suited for cats. Just like you it needs a good mouth cleaning. Unlike you, you'd only have to do it for your cat at least once a week. Make it a part of the grooming-time routine you have with your Scottish Fold.

Bathing Your Scottish Fold

The frequency and necessity for baths of your Scottish Fold will depend on a few factors, like the length of their fur and if they are indoor or outdoor cats.

Scottish Folds who are allowed regular, supervised forays outdoors are advised to have baths at least once a week. This will clear its fur of anything it may have picked up whilst at play outdoors. In the event of your cat getting paint on its fur, avoid using turpentine or any other chemicals on its skin to wipe off the paint. The cats nature of "cleaning" itself is an innate trait of all cats and you don't want it inhaling or ingesting toxic fumes or harmful chemicals. It is best to give your cat a warm bath instead.

Those who are kept indoors need not have as frequent baths and can be given one every fortnight.

Gently introduce it to warm water by dropping a few droplets onto its paw. Cup your hands and gently wet the feet, underside and bottom of your cat. Lather soap in your hands and gently rub your Scottish Fold until the soap is a mild lather. Remember to use soap which is pet-approved when giving your Scottish Fold a bath.

Be sure to thoroughly dry them after the bath and those they are not walking around damp. This may cause them to catch cold and that would be something that can be avoided.

Recommended Vaccinations for Scottish Fold Cats

Like other cat breeds, Scottish Folds, as healthy as they are, can still catch different bacterial and viral infections once in a while; fortunately it can be prevented through vaccination. Core Vaccines are highly recommended if the risk of your cat contracting these diseases is high.

In addition, vaccines are available to offer protection from other potential dangerous diseases like feline leukemia and other fatal virus.

The vaccination recommendations listed below for your cat highly depends on the availability in your area, your cat's age, and any other risk factors specific to its lifestyle:

- **Panleukopenia**
  Class: Core
  Efficacy: High
  Length of Immunity: More than 1 year
  Risk/Severity of Adverse Effects: Low to Moderate

- **Rhinotracheitis**

  Class: Core

  Efficacy: High; reduces severity but not prevent disease

  Length of Immunity: More than 1 year

  Risk/Severity of Adverse Effects: Low

  Remarks: Use intranasal vaccine for faster protection

- **Calicivirus**

  Class: Core

  Efficacy: Variable; reduces severity but not prevent diseases

  Length of Immunity: More than 1 year

  Risk/Severity of Adverse Effects: Low

  Remarks: May see sneezing in cats

- **Rabies**

  Class: Core

  Efficacy: High

  Length of Immunity: Depends on the type of vaccine

  Risk/Severity of Adverse Effects: Low to Moderate

  Remarks: Lower for recombinant vaccines

- **Feline Leukemia**

  Class: Recommended

  Efficacy: Variable

Length of Immunity: Needs revaccination

Risk/Severity of Adverse Effects: Vaccine-related sarcoma can develop with killed vaccines

Remarks: Vaccine is not recommended for cats with minimal or no risk

- **Chlamydophila**

  Class: Non-Core

  Efficacy: Low

  Length of Immunity: Less than 1 year

  Risk/Severity of Adverse Effects: High

  Remarks: Vaccine is not recommended for cats with minimal or no risk

- **Feline Infectious Peritonitis**

  Class: Non-Core

  Efficacy: Low

  Length of Immunity: Unknown

  Risk/Severity of Adverse Effects: Unknown

  Remarks: Not recommended but can be ideal

- **Bordetella**

  Class: Non-Core

  Efficacy: Low

  Length of Immunity: Short

  Risk/Severity of Adverse Effects: More severe in kittens

- **Giardia**

  Remarks: Not recommended, upon advised by the veterinarian

- **Feline Immunodeficiency Virus**

  Remarks: Not recommended unless your cat has been identified with FIV. Upon advised of the veterinarian.

Vaccination Schedule for Cats and Kittens

For kitten aged 6 - 7 weeks old, combination of vaccines, which is consists of feline distemper, rhinotracheitis, and calicivirus is needed. For kittens that are 10 weeks old, combination of vaccines is needed plus Chlamydophila or Pneumonitis, because during this age, they are prone to respiratory diseases.

For kittens that are 12 - 13 weeks old and up (age may vary according to local law), generally they need to have a rabies vaccine as well as feline leukemia vaccine (FeLV), because at this age kittens can be exposed to feline leukemia virus, these vaccines can be given by your local veterinarian.

For adult cats, aside from combination of vaccines booster, cats also need Chlamydophila or Pneumonitis vaccine, feline leukemia vaccine (FeLV), as well as rabies vaccine.

Consult with your local veterinarian to determine the appropriate vaccination schedule for your cat. Remember, recommendations vary depending on the age, breed, and health status of the cat, the potential of the cat to be exposed to the disease, the type of vaccine, whether the cat is used for breeding, and the geographical area where the cat lives or may visit.

Signs of Possible Illnesses

- **Sneezing** - does your cat have nose discharge?
- **Dehydration** - does your cat drink less than the usual? It may be a sign that there is something wrong with your cat
- **Obesity -** is your cat showing signs of obesity? It may be prone to a heart disease, or diabetes. Monitor your cat's weight before it's too late.
- **Elimination** - does your cat regularly urinate and defecate? Always check its litter to make sure that its stool and urine is normal. Contact the vet immediately if there are any signs of bleed and diarrhea.
- **Vomiting** - does your cat vomits and is it showing signs of appetite loss?

- **Coat -** does its coat and skin still feels soft, fluffy and rejuvenated? If your cat is sick sometimes, it appears physically on its body.
- **Paws/Limbs -** does your cat have trouble walking or is it only dragging its legs? It could be a sign of paralysis.
- **Eyes -** are there any discharge in the eyes?
- **Overall Physique -** does your cat stays active or are there any signs of weakness and deterioration?

Emergency Guide

Sometimes no matter how prepared you are or how well you take care your cat, accidents may still happen. In this section you'll be guided on how to prepare if an unforeseen situation occurs. You will learn some tips on how to better handle your cat if an emergency does arise.

a.) Signs of Injuries

The following may signal that your Scottish Fold cat needs immediate medical attention:

- Is there a lump on your cat's skin?
- Is your cat seems unusually short-of-breath?
- Does your cat experience a sudden loss of appetite?
- Have you notice your cat rapidly losing its weight?

- Does your cat drinks often and urinates more frequently than usual?

Seek your veterinarian as soon as you see these signs.

b.) What To Do In Case of Bleeding

The following areas are pressure points on your Scottish Fold cat which, along with direct pressure on the wound, will help stop bleeding.

- Press the upper inside of the front legs to help control bleeding of the lower forelegs.
- Press the upper inside of the rear legs to help control bleeding of the lower hind legs.
- Press the underside of the tail to help control bleeding of the tail.

Important Note:

Do not use a tourniquet. There are a lot of cat limbs lost because the blood supply is cut off for too long.

c.) Signs of Internal Bleeding:

Here are some signs that your cat might be bleeding internally:

- Blood in the vomit
- Blood in the urine

- Pale pink or white gums

If your cat's gums don't turn pink after pressing it, contact your veterinarian as soon as possible.

d.) How to Test Your Cat for Dehydration

Gently lift the skin along its back. Normally, it will snap back into place, if it stayed up in a ridge, which is a sign that your cat is dehydrated because the skin loses elasticity. If this happens, it's an emergency! Contact your veterinarian immediately.

e.) Things You Need In Case of Emergency

These are the things you need to include as part of your first-aid kit in case your cat is injured.

- Gauze rolls
- Absorbent cotton
- Hydrogen peroxide
- Eyewash
- Tweezers
- Syringe (for giving oral medications)
- Clean, white sock (to slip over an injured paw)
- Veterinarian's phone number

f.) Checking Your Cat's Pulse

The normal pulse of cats is anywhere between 110 to 170 beats per minute. Simply feel on the inside of his back thigh, where the leg joins the body and start counting to check your cat's pulse.

Scottish Folds' Care Sheet

You have come to the end of this book. By now it is hoped that this book has shed clearer light and has allowed you a closer look and got to know the sweet Scottish Fold cat a little more. Now that you've learnt what it would take for you as caregiver to be guardian of a Scottish Fold Cat we hope you have come closer to making a decision of taking in or buying a Scottish Fold.

We hope this book which was aimed to enlighten you, the reader, of what to expect when considering a Scottish Fold Cat has done just that. We encourage you to do further research and ask experienced guardians, neighborhood vets and registered breeders of good repute more about the Scottish Fold. Another good thing about networking with other Scottish Fold guardians is the precious exchange of best practices.

Keep in mind however that each cat no matter what pedigree or breed has its own distinct traits, characteristics, personality and behavior. What may be good for one may not necessarily be good for another. Remember that time will play a part in you and your Scottish Fold getting to know each other.

The last chapter of this book gives you an overview of the things you need to remember and apply when you and your household collectively decide to become caregivers and guardians to your very own Scottish Fold Cat.

Here is a quick, last once over of important information to take away. We hope that you enjoy many days of warm cuddling and endless joy as you bring home your very own amiably docile, cuddly, wide-eyed, affectionate and amusingly rotund Scottish Fold Cat.

- **Scientific Name** - Felis catus

- **Pedigreed** - Scottish Fold Cat, Highland Fold and Longhair Fold

- **Appearance:** ears are usually folded toward its head, giving it a rotund-appearance, it sports big expressive eyes

- **Breed**: medium sized feline

- **Height**: 16-18 cm

- **Weight**: Males, 9-13 lbs., Females 6-9 lbs.

- **Physique:** limbs appear roundish, tail should ideally taper.

- **Coat Length**: depends on kind, some sport short fur others have longer fur.

- **Coat Texture**: soft and smooth

- **Colour**: comes in various shades from white, black, smoky gray, two-colours, multi-coloured

- **Tail**: Gentle management and care is to be taken when handling this cat's tail; it should be and appear tapered. A tapered tail shows it is least likely to be prone to genetic disorders

- **Temperament**: Scottish Folds thrive on companionship and gentle play, it loves the company of its humans and other feline-friendly pets, and it is mild-mannered and has a soft voice.

- **Child-friendly**: a resounding yes, as long as you too remind children in your home that it is to be handled gently

- **Other Pets**: research on cat-friendly pets and find out if your present pet would get on well with a Scottish Fold addition

- **Exercise Needs**: Include gentle playtime to your everyday roster

- **Health Condition:** prone to osteodystrophy if both parents have the folded-ear gene. Lifespan is about 13-15 years.

Basic Nutritional Information of the Scottish Fold

- **Nutritional Needs** - diet rich in meats (chicken or beef), grains, oats, egg yolks, protein, calcium from cream cheese, yogurt, buttermilk, iron from liver

- **Water Consumption** - frequent replenishment of water dish is advised

- **Feeding Amount** - varies on specific factors like history, gender, weight, size, age.

- **Feeding Frequency** - It is best to consult with your vet about the amount of food you put out for your cat

- **Mixed Foods** - include allowed veggies like carrots, broccoli into meals

- **Grains** - be sure to include grains and oats in its diet.

Breeding Information

- **Heat period**- two to three weeks
- **Female Sexual Maturity** – 4 -12 months
- **Male Sexual Maturity** - 5 months
- **Female Breeding Age** - 14 months
- **Male Breeding Age** - 16 months
- **Litter Size**- about 4-6 kittens
- **Birth Interval** - 15 – 30 minutes
- **Pregnancy**- 64 - 67 days

Cat Accessories

- Litter boxes
- Cat litter

- Poop scooper, or small plastic pail and shovel
- Scratching posts
- Pet bed
- Blanket

- Travel bag or Cat carrier
- Cat toys

- Feeding bowls
- Brush

- Toothbrush

Index

T

Photo Credits

Page 1 Photo by user karinwoerdehoff via Pixabay.com,
< https://pixabay.com/en/scottish-fold-cat-brit-2094470/ >

Page 15 Photo by user Sophkins via Pixabay.com,
< https://pixabay.com/en/cat-pet-animal-white-cute-kitten-938667/>

Page 25 Photo by user cat-cheng via Pixabay.com,
< https://pixabay.com/en/scottish-fold-cats-cat-pets-animal-1071846/>

Page 36 Photo by user quinntheislander via Pixabay.com,
< https://pixabay.com/en/sleepy-cat-cuddling-domestic-cute-1357008/>

Page 50 Photo by user notoneko via Pixabay.com,
<https://pixabay.com/en/cat-scottish-fold-cat-tower-kitten-1684255/>

Page 57 Photo by user quinntheislander via Pixabay.com,
< https://pixabay.com/en/cat-dark-coffee-lazy-lying-wood-1351612/>

Page 68 Photo by user quinntheislander via Pixabay.com,
< https://pixabay.com/en/fat-cat-lying-floor-wooden-grey-1517449/>

Page 84 Photo by user faerstein via Pixabay.com, < https://pixabay.com/en/manya-scottish-fold-cat-buddha-1755672/>

Page 90 Photo by user cat-cheng via Pixabay.com, < https://pixabay.com/en/scottish-fold-cats-gradient-color-1071855/>

Page 109 Photo by user PublicDomainPictures via Pixabay.com, < https://pixabay.com/en/scottish-fold-breed-cat-cat-kitten-216963/>

References

Breeding and Reproduction of Cats - MerckVetManual.com
<http://www.merckvetmanual.com/pethealth/cat_basics/rout
ine_care_and_breeding_of_cats/breeding_and_reproduction
_of_cats.html>

Cat Proofing Your House - HumaneSociety.org
<http://www.humanesociety.org/animals/cats/tips/cat_proofi
ng_your_house.html?credit=web_id103701348>

Cat Breed Profile: Scottish Fold - Petful.com
<http://www.petful.com/cat-breeds/scottish-fold-cat-breed-
profile/>

Cat Tips - HumaneSociety.org
<http://www.humanesociety.org/animals/cats/tips/>

Feline Diet & Nutrition - Pets.Webmd.com
<http://www.pets.webmd.com/cats/guide/diet-nutrition-
feline>

Fold Health Issues - The Scottish Fold
<http://thescottishfold.com/more-about-the-scottish-fold-
breed/scottish-fold-health-issues/>

How to Train a Cat: Tips and Tricks - Purina.com.au
<http://www.purina.com.au/cats/training/train>

Scottish Fold - Wikipedia
<https://en.wikipedia.org/wiki/Scottish_Fold>

Scottish Fold - Petmd.com
<http://www.petmd.com/cat/breeds/c_ct_scottish_fold>

"Scottish Fold Cat Breed Standard" CFA.org
<http://cfa.org/Portals/0/documents/breeds/standards/scottish.pdf>

Scottish Fold Cat Information and Personality Traits - Hillspet.com
<http://www.hillspet.com/en/us/cat-breeds/scottish-fold>

Scottish Fold Osteodystrophy – Vetbook.org
<http://vetbook.org/wiki/cat/index.php?title=Scottish_fold_osteodystrophy>

The Decision to Breed - PetEducation.com
<http://www.peteducation.com/article.cfm>

Tips for a Healthy Cat -Aspca.org
<https://www.petfinder.com/cats/cat-health/tips-healthy-cat/>

Vaccines & Vaccination Schedule for Cats & Kittens - PetEducation.com

<http://www.peteducation.com/article.cfm>

Your Cats Nutritional Needs: A Science-Based Guide for Pet Owners - Nap.edu

<http://nap.edu>

Feeding Baby
Cynthia Cherry
978-1941070000

Axolotl
Lolly Brown
978-0989658430

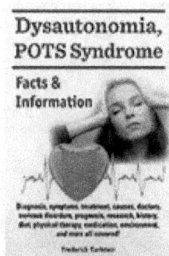

Dysautonomia, POTS
Syndrome
Frederick Earlstein
978-0989658485

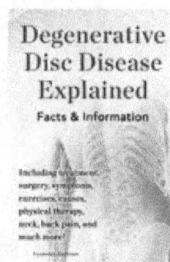

Degenerative Disc
Disease Explained
Frederick Earlstein
978-0989658485

Sinusitis, Hay Fever,
Allergic Rhinitis Explained
Frederick Earlstein
978-1941070024

Wicca
Riley Star
978-1941070130

Zombie Apocalypse
Rex Cutty
978-1941070154

Capybara
Lolly Brown
978-1941070062

Eels As Pets
Lolly Brown
978-1941070167

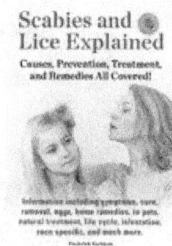

Scabies and Lice Explained
Frederick Earlstein
978-1941070017

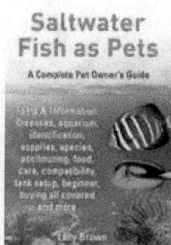

Saltwater Fish As Pets
Lolly Brown
978-0989658461

Torticollis Explained
Frederick Earlstein
978-1941070055

Kennel Cough
Lolly Brown
978-0989658409

Physiotherapist, Physical
Therapist
Christopher Wright
978-0989658492

Rats, Mice, and Dormice
As Pets
Lolly Brown
978-1941070079

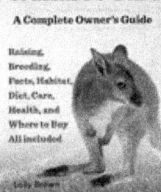

Wallaby and Wallaroo Care
Lolly Brown
978-1941070031

Bodybuilding Supplements
Explained
Jon Shelton
978-1941070239

Demonology
Riley Star
978-19401070314

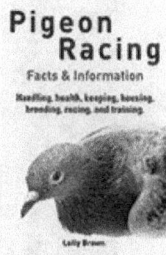

Pigeon Racing
Lolly Brown
978-1941070307

Dwarf Hamster
Lolly Brown
978-1941070390

Cryptozoology
Rex Cutty
978-1941070406

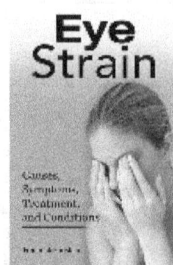

Eye Strain
Frederick Earlstein
978-1941070369

Inez The Miniature Elephant
Asher Ray
978-1941070353

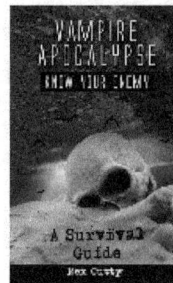

Vampire Apocalypse
Rex Cutty
978-1941070321

www.ingramcontent.com/pod-product-compliance
Lightning Source LLC
La Vergne TN
LVHW051642080426
835511LV00016B/2454